Stress less, Enjoy Life

Stress Less, Live More

Transforming Pressure into Personal Growth

Written By

Dr. Calvin Zeus

Stress less, Enjoy Life

<u>Table Of Contents</u>

Stress less, Enjoy Life

CHAPTER ONE

INTRODUCTION TO STRESS MANAGEMENT

1.1 Understanding Stress

Stress is an inevitable a part of life, and it affects us all in specific places and in distinct ways. It's a herbal response to the needs and pressures we face every day, however know-how strain is going beyond simply acknowledging that it exists. In this bankruptcy, we delve into complicated stress, inspecting its definition, underlying mechanisms, and profound results on our bodies and minds.

What is Stress?

Specifically, stress is the frame's bodily and mental response to perceived threats or demanding situations. This is the alarm device whilst we are faced with conditions that call for more of us than we feel we are able to cope with. Whether it's deadlines at work, monetary problems, dating troubles, or health issues, stress may be resulting from many external and inner elements.

Stress reaction: Fight or flight

When confronted with a stressor, our bodies initiate a "combat or flight" response, a primary survival method designed to accumulate our resources and prepare us for action. These hormones increase coronary heart charge, boom blood strain, sharpen attention, and boom strength stages, permitting us to deal with or break out from perceived hazards.

Types of Stress

Stress is not a one-size-fits-all phenomenon. It manifests in various forms, each with its own unique characteristics and implications for our well-being. Acute stress is the body's immediate response to a sudden threat, like narrowly avoiding a car accident. While this type of stress is short-lived, chronic stress, on the other hand, persists over an extended period, often resulting from ongoing sources of pressure such as work deadlines, financial strain, or relationship problems. Left unchecked, chronic stress can take a significant toll on our physical and mental health.

The Stressors in Our Lives

Stressors come in many shapes and sizes, ranging from major life events like job loss or divorce to daily hassles like traffic jams or technology malfunctions. What constitutes a stressor can vary widely from person to person, as individual differences in personality, coping mechanisms, and life circumstances influence how we perceive and respond to stress. While some stressors may be unavoidable, others may be within our control, highlighting the importance of proactive stress management strategies.

The Mind-Body Connection

While we often think of stress as purely psychological, its effects extend far beyond the realm of our thoughts and emotions. The mind-body connection plays a crucial role in how stress impacts our overall health and well-being. Chronic stress has been linked to a myriad of physical health problems, including cardiovascular disease, digestive disorders, weakened immune function, and even accelerated aging. Moreover, stress can exacerbate existing mental health conditions such as anxiety and depression, perpetuating a vicious cycle of distress.

The Impact of Stress on Daily Life

Stress less, Enjoy Life

The repercussions of stress come and go throughout our daily lives, infiltrating every aspect of our existence. From strained relationships and decreased productivity to disrupted sleep and diminished quality of life, the consequences of unchecked stress can be far-reaching and profound. Recognizing the signs and symptoms of stress is the first step toward regaining control over its influence and reclaiming a sense of balance and resilience.

1.2 Importance Of Stress Management

In the cutting-edge life, stress has become an inevitable companion for lots. From the demands of labor to the pressures of personal relationships, we often find ourselves navigating via a minefield of stressors on each day basis. While a few degree of stress may be motivating and even necessary for boom, unchecked and chronic stress can wreak havoc on our bodily, intellectual, and emotional nicely-being. In this bankruptcy, we delve into the profound significance of pressure control and why it's far important for leading a satisfying and wholesome life.

Stress, in its essence, is the frame's herbal reaction to perceived threats or challenges. This historical survival mechanism, frequently called the "fight or flight" response, triggers a cascade of physiological changes designed to assist us confront or flee from danger. However, in modern day global, where the threats we face are much more likely to be cut-off dates, visitors jams, or economic concerns than predators lurking within the trees, our strain response can emerge as chronically activated, leading to a host of bad consequences.

One of the primary reasons stress management is so crucial is its profound impact on our physical health. Research has shown that chronic stress is associated with a myriad of health problems, including hypertension, heart disease, obesity, diabetes, and weakened immune function. When we are under constant stress, our bodies remain in a state of heightened alertness, with stress hormones like cortisol and adrenaline coursing through our veins. Over time, this sustained elevation in stress hormones can take a toll on our organs and systems, increasing the risk of serious medical conditions. Moreover, the effects of stress extend far beyond the physical realm and can significantly impact our mental and emotional well-being. Prolonged stress has been linked to an increased risk of anxiety disorders, depression, insomnia, and burnout. It can cloud our judgment, impair our memory and concentration, and diminish our overall quality of life. Furthermore, chronic stress can strain our relationships, leading to conflicts and misunderstandings with loved ones, colleagues, and friends.

In addition to its direct effects on health and well-being, stress can also sabotage our productivity and success in various areas of life. When we are overwhelmed by stress, our ability to think clearly, make sound decisions, and solve problems effectively is compromised. We may find ourselves procrastinating, avoiding tasks, or becoming easily distracted, hindering our performance at work, school, or other endeavors. Furthermore, chronic stress can drain our energy and motivation, making it difficult to pursue our goals and aspirations with enthusiasm and vigor.

The importance of stress management lies in its potential to mitigate these detrimental effects and empower us to lead happier, healthier lives. By adopting effective stress management techniques, we can learn to modulate our body's stress response, restore balance to our physiological systems, and cultivate greater resilience in the face of adversity. Whether through relaxation exercises, mindfulness practices, or lifestyle modifications, there are myriad strategies available to help us cope with and reduce stress in our lives. When we prioritize stress management, we not only safeguard our own well-being but also enhance our capacity to support and care for those around us. When we are less burdened by stress, we are better equipped to show up as our best selves in our relationships, both personal and professional. We are more patient, compassionate, and empathetic, fostering deeper connections and a sense of belonging and community.

The importance of stress management cannot be overstated. In a world where stress has become an omnipresent force, learning to go pass its challenges effectively is essential for preserving our health, happiness, and success. By recognizing the profound impact of stress on our lives and taking proactive steps to manage it, we can cultivate resilience, vitality, and a greater sense of well-being.

CHAPTER TWO

CAUSES AND TYPES OF STRESS

2.1 Sources Of Stress

In this our little world, stress seems to be around every corner, waiting to pounce on us when we least expect it. But where does this stress originate? What are the underlying factors that contribute to its relentless grip on our lives?

At the heart of many stressors lie the demands of our professional lives. The workplace can often feel like a pressure cooker, with deadlines looming, expectations mounting, and the constant struggle to maintain a work-life balance. Whether it's the relentless pace of the corporate world, the uncertainty of job security, or the challenges of navigating office politics, our careers can be a significant source of stress. The fear of failure, the pressure to perform, and the constant striving for success can all take a toll on our mental and emotional well-being, leaving us feeling overwhelmed and exhausted.

But stress doesn't stop at the office door. Our personal lives are also fertile ground for tension and strain. Relationships, for instance, can be both a source of support and a source of stress. Whether it's conflicts with family members, disagreements with friends, or the challenges of maintaining a romantic relationship, the dynamics of human interaction can be fraught with emotional landmines. The need for connection and intimacy can clash with feelings of inadequacy, jealousy, or resentment, leading to friction and discord in our closest relationships. And in today's digital age, the constant bombardment of social media, news updates, and virtual connections can further exacerbate feelings of isolation and disconnection, adding another layer of stress to our already overwhelmed minds.

Beyond the confines of our immediate surroundings, external factors also play a significant role in shaping our stress levels. Financial worries, for example, can cast a long shadow over our lives, weighing heavily on our minds and keeping us awake at night. Whether it's the fear of not being able to make ends meet, the burden of debt, or the pressure to keep up with the relentless consumerism of modern society, money matters can be a significant source of stress for many people. And in a world where the gap between the haves and the have-nots seems to widen with each passing day, the constant struggle to keep pace with our peers can fuel feelings of inadequacy and insecurity, adding another layer of stress to our already burdened shoulders.

But perhaps the most insidious source of stress is the one we carry within ourselves: our own thoughts and emotions. The relentless chatter of our inner critic, the endless stream of worries and anxieties, the nagging sense of self-doubt – all these can conspire to keep us trapped in a cycle of negativity and despair. And in a world where success is often equated with busyness and productivity, the pressure to constantly achieve and excel can leave us feeling like we're never doing enough, never measuring up to some elusive standard of perfection.

In conclusion, the sources of stress are as diverse and complicated as the human experience itself. From the pressures of work and relationships to the external forces of society and the internal struggles of our own minds, stress can manifest in many forms, each with its own unique challenges and complexities. But by shedding light on these sources of stress and understanding their underlying dynamics, we can begin to take proactive steps to mitigate their impact on our lives, reclaiming a sense of balance and well-being in an increasingly chaotic world.

2.2 Different Types Of Stress

Acute Stress

Acute stress is the body's natural response to a perceived threat or challenge, triggering a cascade of physiological changes designed to prepare us for action. It is often characterized by its short duration and intense, immediate impact. Imagine a sudden deadline at work, a near-miss accident, or a confrontation with a wild animal, all situations that activate acute stress responses.

In the throes of acute stress, our sympathetic nervous system kicks into high gear, releasing hormones like adrenaline and cortisol. These chemicals sharpen our focus, elevate our heart rate, and increase our energy levels, priming us to confront or escape the perceived danger. This heightened state of arousal is often accompanied by symptoms such as rapid breathing, sweating, and heightened alertness, all indicative of the body's readiness for action.

While acute stress can be uncomfortable and overwhelming in the moment, it serves a vital evolutionary purpose, helping us respond swiftly to immediate threats and navigate challenging situations. However, when acute stress becomes chronic or occurs frequently, it can take a toll on our physical and mental well-being, paving the way for more serious health problems.

Understanding acute stress is essential for recognizing its triggers and implementing effective coping mechanisms. By learning to identify the signs of acute stress and developing strategies to manage its impact, individuals can navigate high-pressure situations with greater resilience and composure, safeguarding their health and well-being in the process.

Chronic Stress

Unlike acute stress, which arises in response to immediate threats, chronic stress is characterized by its persistent, long-term nature. It often emerges in the context of ongoing challenges or unrelenting stressors, such as financial difficulties, job insecurity, or dysfunctional relationships. Unlike acute stress, which activates the body's fight-or-flight response for brief periods, chronic stress keeps the body in a state of prolonged arousal, wreaking havoc on both physical and mental health.

One of the defining features of chronic stress is its insidious nature, it creeps into our lives gradually, often going unnoticed until its effects become impossible to ignore. Over time, the persistent activation of the body's stress response takes a toll on various physiological systems, contributing to a host of health problems ranging from cardiovascular disease and gastrointestinal disorders to weakened immune function and increased susceptibility to infections.

Moreover, chronic stress exerts a profound impact on mental health, fueling feelings of anxiety, depression, and burnout. Prolonged exposure to stress hormones like cortisol can impair cognitive function, disrupt sleep patterns, and erode our resilience in the face of adversity. Left unchecked, chronic stress can become a pervasive force, undermining our quality of life and diminishing our capacity to cope with life's challenges.

Recognizing the signs of chronic stress is the first step toward reclaiming control over our well-being. By acknowledging the sources of chronic stress in our lives and implementing targeted interventions to address them, we can mitigate its harmful effects and cultivate a greater sense of balance and resilience. From mindfulness practices and relaxation techniques to seeking social support and making lifestyle changes, there are myriad strategies available for managing chronic stress and safeguarding our health and happiness in the long run.

CHAPTER THREE

THE IMPACT OF STRESS ON HEALTH

3.1 Physical Effect Of Stress

Stress triggers a cascade of physiological reactions designed to help us address perceived threats. The notorious "combat or flight" reaction, orchestrated with the aid of our sympathetic worried system, floods our bodies with hormones like adrenaline and cortisol. While this response is crucial for survival in acute situations, chronic pressure can cause sustained elevation of those strain hormones, wreaking havoc on our fitness.

Chronic activation of the stress reaction has been connected to a myriad of damaging physical effects, starting from cardiovascular problems along with high blood pressure and coronary heart sickness to gastrointestinal disturbances like irritable bowel syndrome. Understanding the physiological mechanisms at play is vital for greedy the total impact of pressure on our bodies.

Our cardiovascular gadget bears a heavy burden in the face of chronic stress. Prolonged exposure to stress hormones can cause multiplied heart fee and blood stress, placing pressure on the coronary heart and blood vessels. Over time, this can make a contribution to the development of situations together with atherosclerosis, wherein arteries turn out to be narrowed and hardened due to plaque buildup.

Furthermore, stress can exacerbate existing cardiovascular issues, such as arrhythmias and coronary artery disease, and may increase the risk of experiencing cardiac events like heart attacks and strokes. By unscrambling the complex chemistry between stress and cardiovascular health, we gain insight into the importance of prioritizing stress management for the sake of our hearts.

Stress has a profound influence on our metabolism, with implications for both our weight and overall health. Cortisol, often dubbed the "stress hormone," plays a central role in regulating metabolism, mobilizing energy reserves to fuel our fight or flight response. However, chronic stress can disrupt this delicate balance, leading to dysregulation of appetite, cravings for high-calorie foods, and alterations in fat distribution.

Moreover, stress-induced changes in metabolism can contribute to weight gain and obesity, which in turn increase the risk of developing conditions such as type 2 diabetes and metabolic syndrome. By shedding light on the complicated relationship between stress and metabolism, we underscore the importance of adopting holistic approaches to stress management that encompass both physical and mental well-being.

3.2 Psychological Effects Of Stress

When faced with stressors, our brains trigger a cascade of physiological responses, releasing hormones like cortisol and adrenaline. These stress hormones influence our cognitive functions and emotional well-being. Chronic stress can disrupt the delicate balance of neurotransmitters in our brains, leading to mood disorders such as anxiety and depression. Moreover, prolonged exposure to stress can weaken our immune systems, making us more susceptible to illnesses. By unraveling the intricate relationship between stress and our physiological responses, we gain valuable insights into how stress can affect our psychological health.

Stress has a profound effect on our cognitive abilities, shaping how we perceive and process information. Under stress, our attention becomes narrow, focusing solely on the perceived threat at hand while disregarding peripheral cues. This tunnel vision not only impairs our decision-making skills but also hampers our problem-solving abilities. Moreover, chronic stress can hinder our memory formation and retrieval, leading to forgetfulness and cognitive decline over time. The relentless barrage of stressors can overwhelm our cognitive resources, leaving us feeling mentally exhausted and emotionally drained. By recognizing the cognitive impact of stress, we can adopt strategies to enhance our cognitive resilience and preserve our mental faculties in the face of adversity.

At its core, stress is an emotional experience that can leave us feeling overwhelmed, anxious, and vulnerable. Whether it's the pressure to meet societal expectations or the fear of failure, stress can evoke a wide range of emotions that color our perceptions of the world around us. Chronic stress can exacerbate existing emotional vulnerabilities, amplifying feelings of sadness, anger, and despair.

Also, prolonged stress can damage our self-awareness and self-worth, triggering a vicious cycle of negative thoughts and feelings. It is important to recognize the emotional damage stress can cause to our mental health and find positive coping mechanisms to get through turbulent times . By strengthening emotional resilience, we can weather life's storms with grace and dignity, emerging stronger and more resilient than ever before.

3.3 Long-term Consequences of Untreated Stress

Beyond its physical ramifications, untreated stress exacts a heavy toll on our cognitive faculties. Prolonged exposure to stress hormones impairs neuroplasticity, the brain's ability to adapt and reorganize. This impedes learning, memory formation, and problem-solving skills, leading to cognitive decline over time. Moreover, chronic stress is complicatedly linked to the development of neurodegenerative diseases, including Alzheimer's and dementia. As the mind struggles to cope with the incessant demands of stress, its resilience wanes, leaving it vulnerable to the ravages of age-related decline.

Unchecked stress doesn't just affect our bodies and minds; it also erodes our emotional well-being, casting a shadow over our lives. Persistent stressors chip away at our resilience, leaving us vulnerable to mood disorders such as depression and anxiety. The incessant barrage of negative emotions takes its toll on our relationships, leading to increased conflict and isolation. Left unaddressed, chronic stress can rob us of the joy and vitality that once defined our existence, leaving us mired in a state of perpetual distress.

In conclusion, the long-term consequences of untreated stress are broad and sinister, affecting every aspect of our lives. From the silent erosion of our physical health to the gradual dimming of our cognitive faculties and the pervasive cloud of emotional turmoil, the toll of chronic stress is undeniable.

CHAPTER FOUR

Stress Assessment and Identification

4.1 Assessing Your Stress Levels

Stress can often sneak up on us, manifesting in subtle ways that we may not immediately recognize. Self-reflection is the first step in assessing your stress levels. Take a moment to pause and introspect. Consider the different areas of your life: work, relationships, health, and personal goals. How do you feel in each of these domains? Are there recurring patterns of tension or unease? By increasing your self-awareness, you can pinpoint specific stressors and their triggers.

Example: Close your eyes and take a few deep breaths. Think about your typical day, from the moment you wake up to when you go to bed. Notice any moments of frustration, anxiety, or overwhelm. Jot down these instances in a journal to track your stress patterns over time.

Stress doesn't just affect our minds, it also takes a toll on our bodies. Physical symptoms such as headaches, muscle tension, digestive issues, and fatigue are common manifestations of stress. Create a checklist of physical symptoms associated with stress and assess how frequently you experience them. This checklist can serve as a valuable tool for identifying when your stress levels are elevated.

Example: Keep a symptom journal where you record any physical discomfort you experience throughout the day. Rate the intensity of each symptom on a scale of 1 to 10. Over time, look for correlations between your stress levels and the prevalence of these symptoms.

Our emotions provide valuable clues about our stress levels. Feelings of irritability, sadness, frustration, or being overwhelmed are often indicators that stress is present. Conduct an emotional inventory by regularly checking in with your feelings and emotions. Pay attention to any shifts in mood or emotional reactions to different situations.

Example: Set aside a few minutes each day to tune into your emotions. Use a feelings wheel or emotional chart to identify and label your current emotional state. Reflect on the events or circumstances that may have contributed to these feelings.

Several validated tools and questionnaires are available to assess stress levels more systematically. These tools typically consist of a series of questions designed to measure various aspects of stress, including its frequency, intensity, and impact on different areas of life. Consider using one of these tools to gain a more objective understanding of your stress levels.

Example: Take an online stress assessment questionnaire or download a stress-tracking app. Answer the questions honestly and thoughtfully. Review the results to identify areas where you may need to focus your stress management efforts.

4.2 Recognizing Signs and Symptoms of Stress

Stress speaks to us in many for forms and variety of signals, some overt, others masked beneath the surface. It's a language of the body and mind, communicating our internal struggles and external pressures. By learning to interpret this language, we acquire understanding of our well-being, ultimately helping us live a good life.

Physical Manifestations: Listening to Your Body

Our bodies are remarkable storytellers, making stress known through physical sensations and symptoms. From tension headaches to stomach discomfort, palpitations to muscle aches, these bodily cues serve as red flags alerting us to underlying stressors. As we explore these physical manifestations, we develop a deeper awareness of our physiological responses to stress.

Emotional Indicators: The Heart's Silent Ricochets

Emotions are the silent echoes of our hearts, sounding with intensity in times of stress. Anxiety, irritability, sadness, and mood swings are just a few of the emotional indicators that signal our inner turmoil. Yet, amidst the chaos, lies an opportunity for introspection and self-discovery.

Behavioral Clues

Our behaviors often betray the hidden truths of our inner state, offering glimpses into the depths of our subconscious. From changes in appetite and sleep patterns to increased reliance on coping mechanisms such as substance abuse or withdrawal, these behavioral clues provide valuable insights into our psychological well-being. By understanding the little messages encoded within our actions, we gain deeper understanding of the underlying stressors driving our behavior.

CHAPTER FIVE

Coping Strategies for Stress Management

5.1 Relaxation Techniques

Symphony of Breath

Picture this: you're caught in the throes of a stressful day, your mind racing at a million miles per hour. Inhale, Exhale. With each deliberate breath, you invite a sense of serenity to wash over you. Deep breathing, often overlooked in its simplicity, holds the key to unlocking a world of calmness within.

Deep breathing, also known as diaphragmatic breathing, involves inhaling deeply through the nose, allowing the abdomen to expand fully, and exhaling slowly through the mouth. This intentional act of breathing engages the parasympathetic nervous system, triggering the body's relaxation response. As oxygen floods your bloodstream, tensions dissolve, and clarity emerges.

Stress less, Enjoy Life

Let's embark on a journey inward, exploring various deep breathing techniques tailored to suit your needs. From the rhythmic cadence of square breathing to the grounding presence of 4-7-8 breathing, each technique serves as a gateway to tranquility in its own right.

Progressive Muscle Relaxation

Tension manifests not only in the mind but also in the body, weaving its way into the fibers of our muscles like invisible threads of stress. Enter progressive muscle relaxation, a simple yet profoundly effective technique for undoing the webs of tension that bind us.

Developed by American physician Edmund Jacobson in the early 20th century, progressive muscle relaxation involves systematically tensing and releasing different muscle groups, one at a time. As you surrender to the gentle rhythm of tension and release, a wave of relaxation cascades throughout your entire being, melting away stress with each deliberate contraction. From the crown of your head to the tips of your toes,

Through guided imagery and mindful awareness, you'll learn to discern between tension and relaxation, reclaiming control over your physical state. As the practice unfolds, you'll emerge not only rejuvenated but also equipped with a newfound sense of embodiment. Through the union of breath and body, you'll cultivate an oasis of tranquility within, a sanctuary to retreat to amidst life's storms.

5.2 Mindfulness and Meditation

Mindfulness is the art of being fully present in the moment, without judgment or attachment to the past or future. It invites us to tune into our thoughts, emotions, and sensations with gentle curiosity, fostering a greater sense of self-awareness and acceptance. In the fast-paced rhythm of modern life, mindfulness acts as a guiding light, illuminating the path towards inner peace and tranquility.

Meditation, on the other hand, serves as a practical tool for harnessing the power of mindfulness. Through dedicated practice, we learn to quiet the restless chatter of the mind and enter into a state of deep relaxation and stillness. Whether seated in silent contemplation or guided through visualization exercises, meditation offers a sanctuary for the soul, allowing us to tap into our innate wisdom and clarity.

But the benefits of mindfulness and meditation extend far beyond mere relaxation. Research has shown that regular practice can lead to a myriad of positive outcomes, ranging from reduced stress and anxiety to improved focus and emotional resilience. By rewiring the neural pathways of the brain, these practices empower us to navigate life's challenges with grace and equanimity, fostering a profound sense of well-being and vitality.

One of the greatest gifts of mindfulness and meditation is their capacity to deepen our connection with ourselves and others. By cultivating a sense of compassion and empathy towards ourselves, we lay the foundation for more meaningful and authentic relationships with those around us. As we learn to approach ourselves and others with kindness and understanding, we create a ripple effect of healing and transformation that extends far beyond our own lives.

Moreover, mindfulness and meditation offer a gateway to the sacred within the mundane. In moments of stillness and silence, we catch glimpses of the divine essence that resides within each of us, reconnecting us to the vast tapestry of existence. Whether gazing upon the beauty of a sunset or savoring the simple pleasure of a warm cup of tea, these practices invite us to embrace the fullness of life with open arms and an open heart.

5.3 Exercise and Physical Activity

Exercise and physical activity are not just about maintaining physical fitness; they are integral components of a holistic approach to stress management and overall well-being. We will explore the multiple benefits of exercise, debunk common myths, and provide practical tips to help you incorporate physical activity into your daily routine.

Regular physical activity offers a plethora of benefits for both the body and mind. From improving cardiovascular health to boosting mood and most importantly reducing stress, exercise is a potent tool for enhancing overall quality of life. Research has shown that even small amounts of exercise can have significant positive effects on mental health, including reducing symptoms of anxiety and depression.

Now, it's essential to address common myths and misconceptions that may be barriers to getting started. Contrary to popular belief, exercise doesn't have to be grueling or time-consuming to be effective. With the right approach, anyone can reap the rewards of physical activity, regardless of age, fitness level, or lifestyle.

Embarking on a new exercise regimen can feel daunting, but it doesn't have to be overwhelming. Start by setting realistic goals and gradually increasing the intensity and duration of your workouts. Choose activities that you enjoy, whether it's jogging, swimming, dancing, or practicing yoga. Incorporating physical activity into your daily routine, such as taking the stairs instead of the elevator or going for a brisk walk during your lunch break, can also make a significant difference.

Staying motivated to exercise can be challenging, especially when life gets busy or unexpected obstacles arise.

However, by identifying your personal motivations and addressing potential barriers in advance, you can set yourself up for success. Surround yourself with supportive friends or family members, join a fitness class or community sports team, and reward yourself for achieving milestones along the way.

The key to long-term success with exercise is consistency. Rather than viewing physical activity as a chore, strive to make it an enjoyable and integral part of your daily life. Experiment with different types of exercise to keep things interesting, and listen to your body's cues to avoid overtraining or burnout.

CHAPTER SIX

Time Management And Organization

6.1 Prioritizing Tasks

Ah, the timeless struggle of sorting through your never-ending to-do list. It's like playing Tetris with deadlines, but fear not, brave task conquerors!

First things first, let's debunk the myth that multitasking is the ultimate productivity hack. Spoiler alert: it's not. In fact, attempting to juggle multiple tasks simultaneously is like trying to ride a unicycle while juggling flaming torches – it's impressive in theory, but in reality, it's a recipe for disaster. Instead, focus on tackling one task at a time, starting with the most critical or time-sensitive one. Trust me, your sanity will thank you later.

Now, onto the fun stuff – prioritization techniques! Ever heard of the Eisenhower Matrix? It's like a superhero utility belt for your task management woes. Picture this: a grid divided into four quadrants based on urgency and importance. Your mission, should you choose to accept it, is to categorize your tasks accordingly. From the mighty "Do First" quadrant for urgent and important tasks to the humble "Delegate" quadrant for those that can be outsourced to sidekicks (I mean, colleagues), the Eisenhower Matrix is your trusty ally in the battle against task overload.

But wait, there's more! Introducing the ABCDE method, the alphabet soup of prioritization strategies. Here's the gist: assign each task a letter from A to

E based on its level of importance, with A being top priority and E being, well, expendable. By ranking your tasks in order of importance, you'll ensure that you're focusing your time and energy where it matters most. Plus, it's a great excuse to indulge your inner grade-schooler and bust out the colorful highlighters.

And let's not forget about good old-fashioned time blocking, the OG of productivity hacks. Think of it as scheduling playdates for your tasks –

except instead of finger painting and snack time, you're carving out dedicated chunks of time to tackle specific tasks. Whether it's a power hour for plowing through emails or a zen zone for deep work, time blocking helps you structure your day like a boss and keep distractions at bay.

But hey, prioritizing tasks isn't just about checking boxes and crossing off to-dos. It's about reclaiming your time, taking control of your workload, and unleashing your inner task-master extraordinaire. So, go forth, brave prioritizers, and may your to-do lists tremble in awe at your newfound prioritization prowess.

6.2 Setting Realistic Goals

Goal-setting, the cornerstone of every epic quest and the roadmap to greatness. It's crucial to set goals that are not only ambitious but also, dare I say it, achievable.

Let's talk about why setting realistic goals is so darn important. Sure, aiming for the stars is admirable, but if you're trying to launch a rocket with a slingshot, you're gonna have a bad time. Realistic goals are like sturdy stepping stones that lead you to your ultimate destination, they provide structure, direction, and a healthy dose of reality to keep your feet firmly planted on the ground.

Now, let's get down to brass tacks, how do you actually set realistic goals? **Step one:** get clear on what you want to achieve. Whether it's landing your dream job, running a marathon, or mastering the art of the perfect pancake flip, clarity is key. **Step two:** break your big, hairy, audacious goals down into smaller, bite-sized chunks. Think of them as mini-quests on your epic journey, each one bringing you closer to victory.

But here's the kicker – realistic goals aren't just about what you want to achieve; they're also about when and how you're going to achieve them. That's where the magic of SMART goals comes in. SMART stands for Specific, Measurable, Achievable, Relevant, and Time-bound – in other words, the superhero squad of goal-setting criteria. So, before you declare your intentions to the universe, ask yourself: are my goals SMART enough to withstand the trials and tribulations of the quest ahead?

Now, let's talk strategy. One surefire way to set yourself up for success is to focus on what you can control. Sure, you can't control the weather or the stock market (unless you have a secret weather machine or a crystal ball tucked away somewhere), but you can control your actions, your attitude, and your approach to challenges. So, instead of obsessing over external factors, channel your energy into mastering your craft, cultivating resilience, and embracing the journey, bumps and all.

But here's the secret sauce to setting realistic goals: flexibility. Life is like a Choose Your Own Adventure book – full of unexpected twists, turns, and plot twists. So, while it's important to have a clear vision of where you're headed, it's equally important to remain open to new opportunities, course corrections, and alternate endings. After all, the journey is just as important as the destination – if not more so.

So, there you have it – the ultimate guide to setting realistic goals like a boss. Remember, the path to success is paved with determination, grit, and the occasional detour. So, dream big, aim high, and above all, believe in yourself. The world is your oyster, my friend – now go out there and crack it open.

6.3 Effective Time Management Techniques

Time management, the holy grail of productivity hacks and the secret sauce of successful people everywhere. But fear not, my time-strapped comrades, for I come bearing the gift of time management techniques so potent, they'll make even the busiest of bees look like slackers. So, strap in and prepare to level up your time management game like never before!

Let's kick things off with time blocking, the superhero of scheduling techniques. Picture this: your day is a blank canvas, and you're the master artist, painting each hour with purpose and precision. By carving out dedicated time slots for different tasks and activities, you create a structured framework that guides your day with military-like precision. Whether it's a power hour for plowing through emails or a zen zone for deep work, time blocking ensures that you make the most of every precious minute.

But wait, there's more! Prioritization is the name of the game when it comes to effective time management. With techniques like the Eisenhower Matrix and the ABCDE method in your arsenal, you'll become a prioritization ninja, slicing through your to-do list with ruthless efficiency. From must-do tasks to nice-to-have projects, you'll know exactly where to focus your time and energy for maximum impact.

And let's not forget about setting SMART goals – because let's face it, vague goals are so last year. With SMART goals, you'll transform your dreams into actionable targets, complete with deadlines and milestones to keep you on track. Whether you're aiming for a promotion, launching a side hustle, or finally mastering that guitar solo,

SMART goals provide the roadmap to success, one milestone at a time.

Next up, time tracking, because knowledge is power, especially when it comes to how you spend your precious minutes. With time tracking tools at your disposal, you'll gain valuable insights into your productivity habits, identifying time vampires and productivity pitfalls before they suck you dry. Whether it's a simple timer or a sophisticated productivity app, time tracking puts you in the driver's seat of your productivity journey.

And the last, batching and bundling tasks – because let's face it, multitasking is so last decade. By grouping similar activities together and tackling them in focused bursts, you'll minimize distractions and maximize efficiency like never before. Whether it's batching emails, bundling errands, or clustering meetings, this technique ensures that you make the most of your time, one batch at a time.

So, what are you waiting for? It's time to take control of your schedule and conquer the world, one productive minute at a time.

CHAPTER SEVEN

CREEATIVITY AND RELAXATION ACTIVITIES

7.1 Art Therapy

Art therapy, the realm where paintbrushes become wands and canvases transform into portals to the soul. In this enchanted land of creativity and catharsis, we journey through the labyrinth of our minds, armed with nothing but a palette of colors and a heart full of emotions.

But what exactly is art therapy, you ask? Well, my curious friend, it's like therapy, but with a splash of color and a sprinkle of imagination. Instead of spilling your guts to a therapist, you spill your feelings onto a canvas, letting the paint do the talking while you sit back and watch your innermost thoughts come to life before your very eyes.

And the best part? You don't have to be the next Picasso to benefit from art therapy. Whether you're a seasoned artist or you struggle to draw a stick figure, art therapy welcomes you with open arms and a blank canvas, ready to embrace whatever masterpiece you unleash upon it.

So how does it work, you ask? Well, it's simple, really. You pick up a paintbrush, dip it in some colors that speak to your soul, and let your intuition guide your hand as you create. Maybe you start with a swirl of blue that represents the ocean of emotions swirling inside you, or perhaps you opt for a bold splash of red to release the fiery anger burning in your heart.

As you paint, draw, sculpt, or collage, you'll find yourself diving deeper and deeper into the depths of your subconscious, uncovering hidden truths and buried emotions along the way. Each stroke of the brush is like a breadcrumb leading you closer to the heart of your being, offering insights and revelations that words alone could never convey.

And before you know it, you'll emerge from your artistic reverie feeling lighter, freer, and more connected to yourself than ever before. Because in the magical world of art therapy, every stroke is a step towards healing, every color a beacon of hope, and every masterpiece a testament to the resilience of the human spirit.

7.2 Music Therapy

Picture this: you're sitting in a cozy room, surrounded by instruments of every shape and size. The air is alive with the sound of music, as you listen to the gentle strumming of a guitar or the soothing melody of a piano. As the music washes over you, you feel a sense of peace and relaxation settle over your body like a warm blanket on a cold winter's night.

But music therapy is more than just passive listening; it's an active, participatory experience that engages mind, body, and soul. Whether you're drumming out your frustrations on a djembe or belting out your favorite song at the top of your lungs, music therapy invites you to express yourself in ways that words alone cannot.

And the benefits? Oh, they're endless. From reducing anxiety and depression to improving cognitive function and boosting mood, music therapy offers a host of therapeutic benefits that can improve overall quality of life. Whether you're struggling with mental health issues, recovering from physical injury, or simply looking for a creative outlet, music therapy has something to offer everyone.

But perhaps the most magical aspect of music therapy is its ability to connect us with others in a profound and meaningful way. Whether you're making music with a group of strangers or sharing a favorite song with a loved one, music has a way of breaking down barriers and fostering a sense of connection and belonging that transcends language and culture.

So, whether you're strumming a guitar, banging on a drum, or simply singing your heart out, remember this: in the world of music therapy, there are no wrong notes, only opportunities for healing and growth. So let the music play, and let your soul sing.

7.3 Journaling And Writing

Journaling and writing are powerful tools for self-reflection, creativity, and personal growth. Whether you're journaling for self-discovery, creative writing for pleasure, or using writing as a therapeutic tool, these practices offer a variety of benefits that can enhance your mental, emotional, and spiritual well-being.

Journaling is a useful practice that can take many forms, from freeform stream-of-consciousness writing to structured prompts and exercises. By putting pen to paper (or fingers to keyboard), individuals can explore their thoughts, feelings, and experiences in a safe and non-judgmental space. Journaling can help individuals gain clarity, process emotions, and gain insight into themselves and their lives.

One of the key benefits of journaling is its ability to promote self-awareness and introspection. By regularly reflecting on your thoughts and experiences through writing, you can gain a deeper understanding of yourself, your values, and your goals. Journaling can help you identify patterns, clarify your thoughts, and gain perspective on challenging situations, leading to increased self-confidence and self-acceptance.

Additionally, journaling can be a powerful tool for managing stress and improving mental health. Writing about stressful or traumatic experiences can help individuals process and make sense of their emotions, reducing feelings of anxiety and depression. Journaling can also serve as a form of self-care, providing a space for individuals to vent, express gratitude, and practice mindfulness.

Creative writing, on the other hand, offers a different set of benefits. Whether you're writing poetry, fiction, or memoir, engaging in creative writing allows you to tap into your imagination, explore new ideas, and express yourself in a unique and creative way. Creative writing can be a source of joy, inspiration, and fulfillment, offering a creative outlet for self-expression and exploration.

Furthermore, writing can be a therapeutic tool for individuals struggling with mental health issues or traumatic experiences. Writing therapy, also known as expressive writing, involves using writing as a means of processing emotions, confronting difficult memories, and promoting healing. Through guided writing exercises and prompts, individuals can explore their thoughts and feelings in a structured and supportive environment, leading to increased self-awareness and emotional resilience.

CHAPTER EIGHT

SEEKING PROFESSIONAL HELP

8.1 When To Seek Therapy Or Counselling

So how do you know when it's time to take the plunge and seek therapy? Well, for starters, if you find yourself crying more than you laugh, lashing out at loved ones, or struggling to get out of bed in the morning, it's probably time to pick up the phone and make that call. Therapy can provide you with the tools and support you need to cope with overwhelming emotions, manage stress, and regain a sense of control over your life.

But it's not just about the tears and tantrums; therapy can also be a game-changer for those pesky relationship issues that just won't seem to go away. Whether you're fighting with your significant other, clashing with coworkers, or feeling disconnected from friends and family, therapy can help you navigate the rocky terrain of interpersonal relationships with grace and ease.

And let's not forget about those major life transitions and stressors that have a way of knocking us off our feet when we least expect it. Whether you're going through a messy breakup, dealing with a death in the family, or facing financial hardship, therapy can provide you with the support and guidance you need to weather the storm and come out stronger on the other side.

But perhaps the most compelling reason to seek therapy is when you find yourself engaging in harmful or self-destructive behaviors that are putting your health and well-being at risk. Whether it's substance abuse, self-harm, or reckless behavior, therapy can help you identify the underlying issues driving these behaviors and develop healthier coping mechanisms to replace them.

In the end, therapy is not a sign of weakness; it's a sign of strength and courage. So, if you find yourself struggling to keep your head above water, don't be afraid to reach out for help. Therapy can provide you with the support, guidance, and tools you need to get past life's challenges with grace and resilience. Take a deep breath, pick up the phone, and take that first step towards healing and wholeness.

8.2 Types Of Therapy For Stress Management

Let's start with the oldie but goodie: cognitive-behavioral therapy (CBT). This bad boy has been around the block a few times and for a good reason – it works like a charm. CBT focuses on identifying and challenging those pesky negative thought patterns that fuel our stress and replacing them with more rational and helpful ones. It's like a mental spring cleaning, sweeping away the cobwebs of negativity and leaving you with a sparkling new outlook on life.

But if mindfulness is more your style, then mindfulness-based stress reduction (MBSR) might be right up your alley. This zen-inspired approach combines the ancient practice of mindfulness meditation with modern psychological techniques to help you chill out and find your inner calm. By tuning into the present moment and letting go of those pesky worries about the past and future, MBSR can help you cultivate a sense of peace and serenity that will make even the most stressful situations feel like a walk in the park.

And let's not forget about acceptance and commitment therapy (ACT), the new kid on the block with a whole lot of attitude. ACT is all about embracing your inner weirdo and learning to roll with the punches when life throws you a curveball. By accepting your thoughts and feelings without judgment and taking committed action towards your values and goals, ACT can help you build resilience and bounce back from stress like a boss.

But if you're looking for something a little more intense, dialectical behavior therapy (DBT) might be just what the doctor ordered. Originally developed to treat individuals with borderline personality disorder, DBT is like CBT's badass cousin who isn't afraid to get down and dirty with your deepest, darkest emotions. By teaching you skills like emotion regulation, distress tolerance, and interpersonal effectiveness, DBT can help you navigate the stormy seas of stress with grace and ease.

And last but certainly not least, we have psychodynamic therapy, the OG of therapy approaches. Psychodynamic therapy is like a deep dive into the murky depths of your subconscious, where all your deepest fears and desires lurk. By exploring your past experiences and relationships and uncovering the hidden patterns and dynamics that drive your stress, psychodynamic therapy can help you make peace with your inner demons and emerge stronger and wiser on the other side.

Whether you're a CBT aficionado, a mindfulness maven, or a psychodynamic pioneer, there's a therapy approach out there with your name on it. So why wait? Take the plunge and dive headfirst into the wild and wonderful world of therapy for stress management. Your sanity will thank you.

8.3 Finding a Qualified Mental Health Professional

Let's start with the basics, Credentials and Qualifications. When it comes to finding a therapist, it's essential to ensure that you're dealing with a bona fide mental health professional and not some charlatan masquerading as a healer. Look for therapists who are licensed and certified to practice in your state or country, and be sure to verify their credentials with the appropriate licensing board or professional organization. After all, you wouldn't trust your car to a mechanic without a license, so why trust your mind to a therapist without one?

Next up, experience and specialization. Just like doctors have different specialties, therapists also have areas of expertise and focus. Some therapists specialize in specific issues such as anxiety, depression, or trauma, while others may have expertise in working with particular populations such as children, adolescents, or couples. Finding a therapist who has experience and expertise in addressing your specific concerns can make all the difference in the world when it comes to the effectiveness of your therapy.

But credentials and experience are only part of the equation; you also need to consider the therapist's approach and therapeutic style. Different therapists may use different approaches, such as cognitive-behavioral therapy (CBT), psychodynamic therapy, or mindfulness-based therapy. It's essential to find a therapist whose approach resonates with you and feels like a good fit for your personality and preferences. After all, therapy is a deeply personal journey, and you want to feel comfortable and supported every step of the way.

Of course, practical considerations are also important when it comes to finding a therapist. You'll want to find a therapist who is conveniently located and has availability that fits with your schedule. Additionally, you'll need to consider whether the therapist accepts your insurance or offers sliding scale fees if cost is a concern. After all, therapy can be a significant investment of time and money, so you want to make sure you're getting the most bang for your buck.

Finally, don't be afraid to ask for recommendations from friends, family members, or healthcare providers. Word of mouth is often the best way to find a qualified therapist, as you can trust the opinions of people who know you and your needs. And don't forget to trust your gut instinct – if something doesn't feel right, don't be afraid to keep looking until you find the perfect fit. After all, your mental health is too important to settle for anything less than the best.

THE END